Rosa Sardà   Rosa M. Curto

I Like Getting Dirty
Me gusta ensuciarme

English text by Bernice Randall

LECTORUM
PUBLICATIONS, INC.

Mommy washes my face.

Mami me lava la cara.

Daddy washes my ears.

Papi me lava las orejas.

I'm always getting dirty!

¡Siempre me ensucio!

I like getting dirty when it rains.

Me gusta ensuciarme cuando llueve.

I like getting dirty when I paint.

Me gusta ensuciarme cuando pinto.

I like getting dirty when I play.

Me gusta ensuciarme cuando juego.

I like getting dirty when I water the plants.

Me gusta ensuciarme cuando riego.

I like getting dirty when I help around the house.

Me gusta ensuciarme cuando ayudo en casa.

Mommy gets her hands and face dirty.

Mami se ensucia las manos y la cara.

Daddy gets his shirt and pants dirty.

Papi se ensucia la camisa y los pantalones.

We all get a little dirty sometimes!

¡A veces, todos nos ensuciamos un poco!

I LIKE GETTING DIRTY
ME GUSTA ENSUCIARME

Bilingual Edition

Copyright ©2001 Rosa Sardà y Rosa M. Curto
Copyright ©2001, Combel Editorial, S. A.

Originally published in Spanish under the title
ME GUSTA ENSUCIARME
English translation copyright © 2002 by Lectorum Publications, Inc.

This edition published by arrangement with the original publisher
Combel Editorial, S. A., for the United States and Puerto Rico

ISBN 1-930332-32-7
D.L. M-13989-2002
Printed in Spain

10 9 8 7 6 5 4 3 2